Famous Writer Quotes

Chariss K. Walker

For Wholesale and Library Distribution:
CreateSpace Direct
Attn: Customer Service
4900 Lacross Road
N. Charleston, SC 29406
Fax: (206) 922-5928
Email: info@createspace.com
Website: https://www.createspace.com

ISBN-10: 1515308200
ISBN-13: 978-1515308201

Dedication

To Authors and Writers everywhere, especially those of us who aspire to one day be on this list.

Contents

Acknowledgements

Heartfelt thanks to other websites that made this book possible:

IMDb

BrainyQuotes.com

Goodreads.com

Wikipedia.org

ThisBlogBlank.Wordpress.com

Introduction

This book is a collection of quotes by top best-selling fiction authors around the world who have sold at least 100 million books as of July 2015. Although the author quotes can be Googled, they're now conveniently shared here in one central place. The available quotes— sometimes only one or two—touch on the thoughts and feelings of these prolific writers in hopes that you'll find inspiration and a 'new-to-you' author to read and follow.

William Shakespeare (1564-1616)

Brevity is the soul of wit.

Love all, trust a few, do wrong to none.

It is not in the stars to hold our destiny but in ourselves.

No legacy is so rich as honesty.

If music be the food of love, play on.

A fool thinks himself to be wise, but a wise man knows himself to be a fool.

There is nothing either good or bad but thinking makes it so.

We know what we are, but know not what we may do.

Some are born great, some achieve greatness, and some have greatness thrust upon them.

What's in a name? That which we call a rose by any other name would smell as sweet.

Cowards die many times before their deaths; the valiant never taste of death but once.

All the world's a stage, and men and women merely players: they have their exits and their entrances; and one man in his time plays many parts, his acts being seven ages.

God has given you one face and you make yourself another.

With mirth and laughter let old wrinkles come.

When a father gives to his son, both laugh; when a son gives to his father, both cry.

Listen to many, speak to a few.

We are such stuff as dreams are made on; and our little life is rounded with a sleep.

It is a wise father that knows his own child.

To be, or not to be, that is the question.

There is no darkness but ignorance.

What is past is prologue.

This above all: to thine own self be true.

Agatha Christie (1890-1976)

Very few of us are what we seem.

I like living. I have sometimes been wildly, despairingly, acutely miserable, racked with sorrow, but through it all I still know quite certainly that just to be alive is a grand thing.

One doesn't recognize the really important moments in one's life until it's too late.

Dogs are wise. They crawl away into a quiet corner and lick their wounds and do not rejoin the world until they are whole once more.

The popular idea that a child forgets easily is not an accurate one. Many people go right through life in the grip of an idea which has been impressed on them in very tender years.

Barbara Cartland (1901-2000)

Among men, sex sometimes results in intimacy; among women, intimacy sometimes results in sex.

Danielle Steel (1947-)

Lust is temporary, romance can be nice, but love is the most important thing of all. Because without love, lust and romance will always be short-lived.

Sometimes, if you aren't sure about something, you just have to jump off the bridge and grow your wings on the way down.

A bad review is like baking a cake with all the best ingredients and having someone sit on it.

Harold Robbins (1916-1997)

I won't leave any unfinished manuscripts.

Georges Simenon (1903-1989)

The lake and the mountains have become my landscape, my real world.

The fact that we are... I don't know how many millions of people, yet communication, complete communication, is completely impossible between two of those people, is to me one of the biggest tragic themes in the world.

Sidney Shelton (1917-2007)

There's this sense of excitement because you invent and control the characters. You decide whether they live or die. I find this type of creative process tremendously stimulating.

The Dalai Lama... He is a very wise man of great inner peace who believes that happiness is the purpose of our lives. Through his teachings and leadership, he continues to make this world a better place in which to live.

Try to leave the Earth a better place than when you arrived.

Enid Blyton (1897-1968)

My work in books, films and talks lies almost wholly with children, and I have very little time to give to grown-ups.

Writing for children is an art in itself, and a most interesting one.

Dr. Seuss (1904-1991)

Today you are you! That is truer than true! There is no one alive who is you-er than you!

Don't cry because it's over. Smile because it happened.

You have brains in your head. You have feet in your shoes. You can steer yourself in any direction you choose. You're on your own, and you know what you know. And you are the guy who'll decide where to go.

You're never too old, too wacky, too wild, to pick up a book and read to a child.

Gilbert Patten (1866-1945)

Science seeks truth and discovers rightness. Religion seeks righteousness and discovers truth. Both have acquired knowledge of creative and destructive ways, and both point the same way of right living.

J.K. Rowling (1965-)

It is impossible to live without failing at something, unless you live so cautiously that you might as well not have lived at all, in which case you have failed by default.

I was set free because my greatest fear had been realized, and I still had a daughter who I adored, and I had an old typewriter and a big idea. And so rock bottom became a solid foundation on which I rebuilt my life.

It is our choices... that show what we truly are, far more than our abilities.

It takes a great deal of bravery to stand up to our enemies, but just as much to stand up to our friends.

There are some things you can't share without ending up liking each other.

I sometimes have a tendency to walk on the dark side.

I think you're working and learning until you die.

Never trust anything that can think for itself if you can't see where it keeps its brain.

If you want to see the true measure of a man, watch how he treats his inferiors, not his equals.

Bigotry is probably the think I detest most.

Anything's possible if you've got enough nerve.

'Harry Potter' gave me back self-respect. Harry gave me a job to do that I loved more than anything else.

I would like to be remembered as someone who did the best she could with the talent she had.

Leo Tolstoy (1828-1910)

Everyone thinks of changing the world, but no one thinks of changing himself.

The two most powerful warriors are patience and time.

There is no greatness where there is no simplicity, goodness and truth.

The sole meaning of life is to serve humanity.

All, everything that I understand, I understand only because I love.

Art is not a handicraft, it is the transmission of feeling the artist has experienced.

Music is the shorthand of emotion.

Truth, like gold, is to be obtained not by its growth, but by washing away from it all that is not gold.

All violence consists in some people forcing others, under threat of suffering or death, to do what they do not want to do.

True life is lived when tiny changes occur.

Without knowing what I am and why I am here, life is impossible.

It is amazing how complete is the delusion that beauty is goodness.

All happy families resemble one another, each unhappy family is unhappy in its own way.

If you want to be happy, be.

Corín Tellado (1927-2009)

If Barbara Cartland, Victoria Holt or Jude Deveraux say they like society and inventing romantic stories to live and feel what they attribute to their protagonists, my success lies in the ability to get readers identified with the invented characters, making everyday an adventure in search of love, enveloping its characters in situations of jealousy, fear, friendship.

Jackie Collins (1937-)

Do not copy my style! The first rule of writing is write about what you know, not what you think you know. So, think about what you've done in your life and write about that.

I have written 20 books, and each one is like having a baby. Writing is not easy; some people want to write books but just can't put a story together. I can put together a story that interests both me and my readers.

I really fall in love with my characters, even the bad ones. I love getting together with them. They tell me what to do; they take me on a wild and wonderful trip.

Horatio Alger, Jr. (1832-1899)

The institution of chivalry forms one of the most remarkable features in the history of the Middle Ages.

No period of my life has been one of such unmixed happiness as the four years which have been spent within college walls.

R. L. Stine (1943 -)

Read. Read. Read. Just don't read one type of book. Read different books by various authors so that you develop different styles.

When I write, I try to think back to what I was afraid of or what was scary to me, and try to put those feelings into books.

I always just wanted to be funny. I never really planned to be scary.

I've never turned into a bee – I've never been chased by a mummy or met a ghost. But many of the ideas in my books are suggested by real life.

Dean Koontz (1945 -)

I really believe that everyone has a talent, ability, or skill that he can mine to support himself and to succeed in life.

Like all of us in this storm between birth and death, I can wreak no great changes on the world, only small changes for the better, I hope, in the lives of those I love.

Books were this wonderful escape for me because I could open a book and disappear into it, and that was the only way out of that house when I was a kid.

There's sometimes a weird benefit to having an alcoholic, violent father. He really motivated me in that I never wanted to be anything like him.

Readers will stay with an author, no matter what the variations in style and genre, as long as they get that sense of story, of character, of empathetic involvement.

Sometimes there is no darker place than our thoughts, the moonless midnight of the mind.

If I drive myself to the brink of my ability, then I don't get stale or bored.

Nora Roberts (1950 -)

You don't find time to write. You make time. It's my job.

Love and magic have a great deal in common. They enrich the soul, delight the heart. And they both take practice.

Every single book is a challenge.

Alexander Puskin (1799-1837)

I do not like Moscow life. You live here not as you want to live, but as old women want you to.

Stephen King (1947 -)

The trust of the innocent is the liar's most useful tool.

Monsters are real, and ghosts are real too. They live inside us, and sometimes, they win.

A lot of us grow up and we grow out of the literal interpretation that we get when we're children, but we bear the scars all our life. Whether they're scars of beauty or scars of ugliness, it's pretty much in the eye of the beholder.

We like to think about how smart we are. But I think talent as a writer is hard-wired in, it's all there, at least the basic elements of it. You can't change it any more than you can choose whether to be right handed or left handed.

Fiction is the truth inside the lie.

You cannot hope to sweep someone else away by the force of your writing until it has been done to you.

As a writer, one of the things that I've always been interested in doing is actually invading your comfort space. Because that's what we're supposed to do. Get under your skin, and make you react.

People think that I must be a very strange person. This in not correct. I have the heart of a small boy. It is in a glass jar on my desk.

Every book you pick up has its own lesson or lessons, and quite often, the bad books have more to teach than the good ones.

The most important things are the hardest things to say. They are the things you get ashamed of because words diminish your feelings – words shrink things that seem timeless when they are in your head to no more than living size when they are brought out.

If you don't have the time to read, you don't have the time or tools to write.

Get busy living, or get busy dying.

Louis L'Amour (1908-1988)

Too often I would hear men boast of the miles covered that day, rarely of what they had seen.

No memory is ever alone; it's at the end of a trail of memories, a dozen trails that each have their own associations.

Nobody got anywhere in the world by simply being content.

Victory is won not in miles but in inches. Win a little now, hold your ground, and later, win a little more.

There will come a time when you believe everything is finished. Yet that will be the beginning.

Anger is a killing thing: it kills the man who angers, for each rage leaves him less than he had been before – it takes something from him.

Erie Stanley Gardner (1889-1970)

The real trouble with the writing game is that no general rule can be worked out for uniform guidance, and this applies to sales as well as writing.

After you've written a story, the thing to do is sell it. Sounds simple, and it is, if one will follow certain basic principles of salesmanship.

Jin Yong (1924 -)

Know, you're not going to ever be able see love, you just can feel it

Jiro Akagawa (1948 -)

You'll find that once you've worked at the same place for almost twenty years, no one complains, whatever you do.

Janet Dailey (1944-2013)

Someday is not a day of the week.

Edgar Wallace (1875-1932)

An intellectual is someone who has found something more interesting than sex.

I never followed illusory values, such as success, but I searched and found the strengths that have allowed a broader conception of the world, and ever greater capacity of gratitude to my fellow men and sincere humility that assists me today, while my little vantage point along the path that goes up and never ends, watching with admirable patience and courage of those who are still struggling behind me.

Robert Ludlum (1927-2001)

Characterization is integral to the theatrical experience.

I try as best I can to enter the realm of nuances of human behavior.

Life is extremely complicated.

James Patterson (1947-)

A lot of writers fall in love with their sentences or their construction of sentences, and sometimes that's great, but not everybody is Gabriel Garcia Marquez or James Joyce. A lot of people like to pretend that they are, and they wind up not giving people a good read or enlightening them.

I guess I write four or five hours a day, but I do it seven days a week. It's very disciplined, yes, but it's joy for me.

There are reasons people seek escape in books, and one of those reasons is that the boundary of what can happen is beyond what we do – or would want to see in real life.

Frédéric Dard (1921-2000)

There are several ways to be a fool, but the fool always chooses the worst.

I thought I was an oak; I was in fact an acorn.

This can be explained, but not directly translated.

Jeffrey Archer (1940 -)

I'm passionate again about writing. This is important to me; it's got to be the comeback book.

I feel I have had a very interesting life, but I am rather hoping there is still more to come. I still haven't captained the England cricket team, or sung at Carnegie Hall!

When a book comes out, I wonder if one person will buy it. It's agony. Of course, it's stupid, but it's agony.

Stan and Jan Berenstain (1923-2012)

It's wonderful to do something you love for so many years. Not everyone has that.

They say jokes don't travel well, but family humor does. Family values is what we're all about.

John Grisham (1955 -)

Writing's still the most difficult job I've ever had – but it's worth it.

I was a lawyer for 10 years – a short time, but it molded me into who I am. My clients were little people fighting big corporations, so it was a natural thing to not only represent the little guy but also to pull for him – it's the American way.

There's always such a rush to judgment. It makes a fair trial hard to get.

I have learned not to read reviews. Period. And I hate reviewers. All of them, or at least all but two or three. Life is much simpler ignoring reviews and the nasty people who write them. Critics should find meaningful work.

Zane Grey (1872-1939)

Love grows more tremendously full, swift, poignant, as the years multiply.

I see so much more than I used to see. The effect has been to depress and sadden and hurt me terribly.

Work is my salvation. It changes my moods.

I can write best in the silence and solitude of the night, when everyone has retired.

Irving Wallace (1916-1990)

Every man can transform the world from one of monotony and drabness to one of excitement and adventure.

To be one's self, and unafraid whether right or wrong, is more admirable than the easy cowardice of surrender to conformity.

J.R.R Tolkien (1892-1973)

All that is gold does not glitter, not all those who wander are lost; the old that is strong does not wither, deep roots are not reached by the frost.

If more of us valued food and cheer and song above hoarded gold, it would be a merrier world.

It's the job that's never started as takes longest to finish.

Courage is found in unlikely places.

The wide world is all about you: you can fence yourselves in, but you cannot forever fence it out.

Many children make up, or begin to make up, imaginary languages. I have been at it since I could write.

Do not meddle in the affairs of Wizards, for they are subtle and quick to anger.

You have been chosen, and you must therefore use such strength and heart and wits as you have.

A pen is to me as a beak is to a hen.

Myth and fairy-story must, as all art, reflect and contain in solution elements of moral and religious truth (or error), but not explicit, not in the known form of the primary 'real' world.

Many that live deserve death. And some that die deserve life. Can you give it to them? Then do not be too eager to deal out death in judgment. For even the very wise cannot see all ends.

It may be the part of a friend to rebuke a friend's folly.

Karl May (1842-1912)

I don't care about losing people who don't wanna be in my life anymore. I've lost people who meant the world to me and I'm still doing just fine.

Mickey Spillane (1918-2006)

If you're a singer, you lose your voice. A baseball player loses his arm. A writer gets more knowledge, and if he's good, the older he gets, the better he writes.

C. S. Lewis (1898 – 1963)

Integrity is doing the right thing, even when no one is watching.

We all want progress, but if you're on the wrong road, progress means doing an about-turn and walking back to the right road; in that case, the man who turns back soonest is the most progressive.

Education without values, as useful as it is, seems rather to make man a more clever devil.

The task of the modern educator is not to cut down jungles, but to irrigate deserts.

We are what we believe.

You are never too old to set another goal or to dream a new dream.

Affection is responsible for nine-tenths of whatever solid and durable happiness there is in our lives.

You can't get a cup of tea big enough or a book long enough to suit me.

No one ever told me that grief felt so like fear.

Has this world been so kind to you that you should leave with regret? There are better things ahead than any we leave behind.

Kyotaro Nishimura (1930 -)

My mystery books explore the criminal mind to make people do the unthinkable.

Dan Brown (1964 -)

Well, you know, in any novel you would hope that the hero has someone to push back against, and villains – I find the most interesting villains those who do the right things for the wrong reasons, or the wrong things for the right reasons. Either one is interesting. I love the gray area between right and wrong.

I learned early on not to listen to either critique – the people who love you or the people who don't like you.

I've learned that universal acceptance and appreciation is just an unrealistic goal.

I consider myself a student of many religions. The more I learn, the more questions I have. For me, the spiritual quest will be a life-long work in progress.

The more science I studied, the more I saw that physics becomes metaphysics and numbers become imaginary numbers. The farther you go into science, the mushier the ground gets. You start to say, 'Oh, there is an order and a spiritual aspect to science.

I still get up every morning at 4 A.M. I write seven days a week, including Christmas. And I still face a blank page every morning, and my characters don't really care how many books I've sold.

It's not about what you tell the reader, it's about what you conceal.

Ann M. Martin (1955 -)

I think reading is a gift. It was a gift that was given to me as a child by many people, and now as an adult and a writer, I'm trying to give a little of it back to others. It's one of the greatest pleasures I know.

Rotaro Shiba (1923-1996)

(No quotes found) Shiba is widely appreciated for the originality of his analyses of historical events and many people in Japan have read at least one of his works.

Arthur Hailey (1920-2004)

I set myself 600 words a day as a minimum output, regardless of the weather, my state of mind or if I'm sick or well. There must be 600 finished words- not almost right words.

I don't think I really invented anybody. I have drawn on real life.

Gerard de Villiers (1929-2013)

If you fall off your horse, you have to get back on or you are dead.

I'm not a sex machine; I'm a writing machine.

Intelligence people don't give a damn about civilian lives. They are cold fish.

I don't consider myself a literary man. I'm a storyteller. I write fairy tales for adults. And I try to put some substance into it.

We are all strangled by political correctness.

Beatrix Potter (1866-1943)

Thank goodness I was never sent to school; it would have rubbed off some of the originality.

Believe there is a great power silently working all things for good, behave yourself and never mind the rest.

There is something delicious about writing the first words of a story. You never quite know where they'll take you.

Michael Crichton (1942-2008)

Absence of proof is not proof of absence.

Professor Johnston often said that if you didn't know history, you didn't know anything. You were a leaf that didn't know it was part of a tree.

Richard Scarry (1919-1994)

Wherever I go, I'm watching. Even on vacation, when I'm in an airport or a railroad station, I look around, snap pictures, and find out how people do things.

Clive Cussler (1931 -)

When I first started writing, I was in advertising at the time; I was doing most of my writing on weekends. I had studied most of the other series heroes and I figured it would be fun for mine to be different and put him in and around water. So I dreamed up Dirk Pitt.

Sometimes my plot lines are so convoluted; I get calls from friends at 3 am saying 'you SOB, you'll never pull this one off.'

My friends joke that I raised the Titanic and never left the Rockies.

Alistair MacLean (1922-1987)

I wrote each book in thirty-five days flat – just to get the darned thing finished.

I'm not a born writer, and I don't enjoy writing.

Ken Follett (1949 -)

There is no point in asking a man a question until you have established whether he has any reason to lie to you.

Listen, I wrote 10 unsuccessful books before I broke through, so I'm looking all the time to keep my books fascinating. I want to write what people read, not push any message.

I wake up with the story in my head, so I really like to be at my desk about five minutes after I wake up. So I don't get dressed. I put on a bathrobe; I make tea and sit at my desk.

Astrid Lindgren (1907-2002)

I have never experienced being madly in love the way most people seem to have been, although it is not something I would miss. Instead, I have had an enormous ability to love my children and my grandchildren and my great grandchildren.

I don't mind dying, I'll gladly do that, but not right now, I need to clean the house first.

Debbie Macomber (1948 -)

We all face difficulties of our own, and how comforting it is to immerse yourself in a book – my book, any book, any romance. It's entertainment, it's escape, and it can even be an inspiration.

Romance focuses on emotions and on relationships, both of which are fundamentally important to women.

Paulo Coelho (1947 -)

Waiting is painful. Forgetting is painful. But not knowing which to do is the worst kind of suffering.

Be brave. Take risks. Nothing can substitute experience.

When you want something, all the universe conspires in helping you to achieve it.

Eiji Yoshikawa (1892-1962)

...you're going to find people from all over the country, everyone hungry for money and position. You won't make a name for yourself just doing what the next man does. You'll have to distinguish yourself in some way.

Hold on to your life and make it honest and brave.

Catherine Cookson (1906-1998)

Oh God, I'm sorry I bring trouble on people. I don't mean to, you know that, you know that. And don't punish me by taking Ned. Keep him safe that's all I ask. That's all I'll ever ask again, just keep him safe.

Stephenie Myer (1973 -)

It's easier to come up with new stories than it is to finish the ones you already have. I think every author would feel that way.

Sometimes ideas feel like they are already there, and that you're just discovering them.

Maybe it's because I'm a little naïve, but I do like to think that there aren't really very many truly bad people in the world. I think that everybody has their reasons for what they do, and if you really look through their eyes, you could probably understand them.

Norman Bridwell (1928-2014)

How can you fully open your heart to someone new, when in fact, what you really need is closure from your past.

I feel very fortunate to have this part in teaching children to read.

David Baldacci (1960 -)

As a lawyer, as a private citizen, you see a lot of injustice. You see a lot of people who should have been punished and are not, and people who were punished wrongfully are not vindicated. Fiction is sort of a way to set the record straight, and let people at least believe that justice can be achieved and the right outcomes can occur.

Most people associate reading with lying on the beach. They don't see that it's crucial for a democracy!

Some people take 10 years to write a book and some can do one in under a year.

Roald Dahl (1916-1990)

If my books can help children become readers, then I feel I have accomplished something.

A little nonsense now and then is relished by the wisest of men.

Evan Hunter (1926-2005)

I wanted to be an artist. I was studying art. I wanted to be a great painter. When I went into the Navy, there wasn't much to draw at sea. So I began writing, and I began reading a lot.

Readers are what it's all about, aren't they? If not, why am I writing?

Changing writing styles is like an actor taking on a different part.

Andrew Neiderman (1940 -)

Human misery was the trough from which she now fed herself and she felt more comfortable in the presence of other unlucky people. It made her feel less alone, less diminished.

Roger Hargreaves (1935-1988)

The long-armed orange character who was the first Mr Man began with a question: 'What does a tickle look like?'

Anne Rice (1941 -)

To really ask is to open the door to the whirlwind. The answer may annihilate the question and the questioner.

To write something, you have to risk making a fool of yourself.

Evil is always possible. Goodness is a difficulty.

I feel like an outsider, and I always will feel like one. I've always felt that I wasn't a member of any particular group.

We're frightened of what makes us different.

First-person narrators is the way I know how to write a book with the greatest power and chance of artistic success.

Robin Cook (1940)

If it looks like a duck, quacks like a duck, it's a duck!"

There were no international terrorists in Iraq until we went in. It was we who gave the perfect conditions in which Al Qaeda could thrive.

Nothing great in the world has been accomplished without passion.

Wilbur Smith (1933 -)

Write for yourself, not for a perceived audience. If you do, you'll mostly fall flat on your face, because it's impossible to judge what people want. And you have to read. That's how you learn what is good writing and what is bad. Then the main thing is application. It's hard work.

I think one of the most poignant things is unrequited love and loneliness.

Erskine Caldwell (1903-1987)

Many southern writers must have learned the art of storytelling from listening to oral tales. I did. It gave me the knowledge that the simplest incident can make a story.

To me there is no such thing as creative writing. It's either good writing, whatever the subject, or it's not creative.

All I ever know is the first line, the first sentence, the first page.

I'm not interested in plots. I'm interested only in the characterization of people and what they do.

Eleanor Hibbert (1906-1993)

Never regret. If it's good, it's wonderful. If it's bad, it's experience.

Lewis Carroll (1832-1898)

Sometimes I've believed as many as six impossible things before breakfast.

Who in the world am I? Ah, that's the great puzzle.

She generally gave herself very good advice, (though she very seldom followed it).

Denise Robins (1897-1985)

Suddenly a young man named Ivor Nicholson came along – a clever, charming journalist who, with the wealth of Bernard Watson to back his new venture, launched a new publishing house – Ivor Nicholson & Watson. They wanted my name on their list. They tempted me with what was the biggest offer I had ever received from any literary quarter, a cheque for one thousand pounds, free, gratis, and for which I need do no work. It was merely for signing the contract! I did not go behind Charles Boon's back. I told him the facts. Unfortunately, he was so annoyed by Ivor Nicholson's offer that he refused to compete and at once released me from my contract with his firm. Somewhat reluctantly, I left my old publishers and became the new Nicholson & Watson 'star' author.

Cao Xueqin (1715-1763)

Any doctor will do in an emergency.

Truth becomes fiction when the fiction is true; real become not-real where the unreal's real.

The cunning waste their pains; the wise men vex their brains; but the simpleton, who seeks no gains, with belly full, he wanders free as drifting boat upon the sea.

Ian Fleming (1908-1964)

Once is happenstance. Twice is coincidence. Three times is enemy action.

Writing about 2,000 words in three hours every morning, 'Casino Royale' dutifully produced itself. I wrote nothing and made no corrections until the book was finished. If I had looked back at what I had written the day before, I might have despaired.

I shall not waste my days in trying to prolong them.

Hermann Hesse (1877-1962)

Solitude is independence.

Some of us think holding on makes us strong; but sometimes it is letting go.

Everything becomes a little different as soon as it is spoken out loud.

If you hate a person, you hate something in him that is part of yourself. What isn't part of ourselves doesn't disturb us.

Rex Stout (1886-1975)

I have never regarded myself as this or that. I have been too busy being myself to bother about regarding myself.

There are two kinds of statistics: the kind you look up and the kind you make up.

As a professional writer of detective stories, I string along with the ballplayers. I love a ball game.

I still can't decide which is more fun – reading or writing.

Anne Golon (1921 -)

Angelique, my dear child, love is not what heals us. Love is what burns us. And in you, the flame burns pure and hot.

Frank G. Slaughter (1908-2001)

Seek truth and you will find a path.

Edgar Rice Burroughs (1875-1950)

I loved her. I still love her, though I curse her in my sleep, so nearly one are love and hate, the two most powerful and devastating emotions that control man, nations, life.

John Creasey (1908-1973)

(No quotes found) John Creasey MBE was an English crime and science fiction writer who wrote more than six hundred novels using twenty-eight different pseudonyms.

James A. Michener (1907-1997)

I love writing. I love the swirl and swing of words as they tangle with human emotions.

An age is called Dark not because the light fails to shine, but because people refuse to see it.

I think the crucial thing in the writing career is to find what you want to do and how you fit in. What somebody else does is of no concern whatever except as an interesting variation.

The arrogance of the artist is a very profound thing, and it fortifies you.

The permanent temptation of life is to confuse dreams with reality. The permanent defeat of life comes when dreams are surrendered to reality.

Yasuo Uchida (1934 -)

(No quotes found) A popular Japanese mystery author featuring a brilliant detective Mitsuhiko Asami.

Seiichi Morimura (1933 -)

(No quotes found) Seiichi Morimura is a Japanese novelist and author. He is best known for the controversial The Devil's Gluttony, which revealed the atrocities committed by Unit 731 of the Imperial Japanese Army during the Sino-Japanese War.

Mary Higgins Clark (1927 -)

If you want to be happy for life, love what you do.

The truth is I hate cocktail parties when the only person I know is my supposed date, and he abandons me the minute we come in the door.

Penny Jordan (1946-2011)

Only the weak blame their past for the faults they find in their present; the strong acknowledge the effects of their past and then move on from it. We are all free to choose whether we will be weak or strong.

Patricia Cornwell (1956 -)

I believe the root of all evil is abuse of power.

Survival was my only hope, success my only revenge.

Even if you are a best-seller, you feel insecure because it is all so unpredictable.

Tom Clancy (1947-2013)

I've made up stuff that turned out to be real, that's the spooky part.

Nothing is as real as a dream. The world can change around you, but your dream will not. Your life may change, but your dream doesn't have to. Responsibilities need not erase it. Duties need not obscure it.

Learn to write the same way you learn to play golf. You do it and keep doing it until you get it right.

Life is about learning; when you stop learning, you die.

Leon Uris (1924-2003)

My first book was rejected nine times. It turned out to be a best seller, Battle Cry, in 1953.

Writing basically breaks down to relationships between people and that is what you write about.

I have drawn inspiration from the Marine Corps, the Jewish struggle in Palestine and Israel, and the Irish.

I enjoy writing, sometimes, I think that most writers will tell you about the agony of writing more than the joy of writing, but writing is what I was meant to do.

I essentially write for myself.

Alexandre Dumas (1802-1870)

All human wisdom is summed up in two words: wait and hope.

Only a man who has felt ultimate despair is capable of feeling ultimate bliss.

It is necessary to have wished for death in order to know how good it is to live.

All generalizations are dangerous, even this one.

Nothing succeeds like success.

Rick Riordan (1964 -)

To a degree, the Greek and Roman mythological heroes are just the first superheroes. They appeal to children for much the same reason. These gods and heroes may have powers, but they get angry and they do the wrong thing. They are human too.

It's not easy. I got lots of rejections when I first started out. If you want to write, you have to believe in yourself and not give up. You have to do your best to practice and get better.

I've always liked the idea that writing is a form of travel. And I started my writing career as a mystery novelist for adults.

Charles Dickens (1812-1870)

Have a heart that never hardens, and a temper that never tires, and a touch that never hurts.

The pain of parting is nothing to the joy of meeting again.

It was the best of times; it was the worst of times.

Reflect upon your present blessings of which every man has many – not on your past misfortunes, of which all men have some.

An idea, like a ghost, must be spoken to a little before it will explain itself.

We forge the chains we wear in life.

It opens the lungs, washes the countenance, exercises the eyes, and softens down the temper; so cry away.

Jane Austen—Author (1775–1817)

There is no charm equal to tenderness of heart.

Life seems but a quick succession of busy nothings.

Friendship is certainly the finest balm for the pangs of disappointed love.

Vanity and pride are different things, though the words are often used synonymously. A person may be proud without being vain. Pride relates more to our opinion of ourselves; vanity, to what we would have others think of us.

The person, be it gentleman or lady, who has not pleasure in a good novel, must be intolerably stupid.

Selfishness must always be forgiven you know, because there is no hope of a cure.

Jack Higgins (1929 -)

Words become meaningless; the mind cuts itself off from reality for a little while, a necessary breathing space until one is ready to cope.

I realized fear one morning with the blare of the foxhunter's sound. When they're all chasin' the poor bloody fox, 'tis safer to be dressed like the hound.

Victor Hugo (1802-1885)

Music expresses that which cannot be said and on which it is impossible to be silent.

The greatest happiness in life is the conviction that we are loved: loved for ourselves, or rather, loved in spite of ourselves.

Jules Verne (1828-1905)

Imagine a society in which there were neither rich nor poor. What evils, afflictions, sorrows, disorders, catastrophes, disasters, tribulation, misfortunes, agonies calamities, despair, desolation and ruin would be unknown to man!

If you enjoyed this book, please leave a review for other readers on Amazon, B&N, Goodreads and other book sites. Reviews are important. Thanks!

About the Author

Award winning author, Chariss K. Walker, M.Msc, writes fiction and nonfiction books with a metaphysical message. All of her books are sold worldwide in eBook, paperback, and many are in large print. Chariss lives in Amarillo, Texas. Connect with Chariss on social media sites. She wants to hear from you. Visit her website at www.chariss.com for a complete social media list, including AuthorGraph.

Fiction Books:

my name is tookie
Crescent City (An Alec Winters Series, Book 1)
Port City (An Alec Winters Series, Book 2)
Harbor City (An Alec Winters Series, Book 3)
Kaleidoscope (The Vision Chronicles, Book 1)
Spyglass (The Vision Chronicles, Book 2)
Window's Pane (The Vision Chronicles, Book 3)
Windows All Around (The Vision Chronicles, Book 4)
Open Spaces (The Vision Chronicles, Book 5)
Stream of Light (The Vision Chronicles, Book 6)
Lamp's Light (The Vision Chronicles, Book 7)
Clear Glass (The Vision Chronicles, Book 8)
The Journey
The Retreat

Nonfiction Books:

Famous Writer Quotes
Abundance: Allowing the Universe to Manifest Your Desires
How to Find Us on Facebook
The Spiritual Gifts: Understanding for the Great Shift and Beyond
Chakra Basics: Fundamentals of Spiritual Growth
Make a Joyful Noise: Searching for a Spiritual Path in a Material World
Make a Joyful Noise Study Guide
Love & Sex: A Personal Journey